Dear Wyatt,

May you enjoy & profit in your new home, but always remember the sea & granite of Maine.

Congratulations!

Leigh &
Kit

THE COMPLETE
HOW TO SPEAK SOUTHERN

The Complete
HOW TO SPEAK
SOUTHERN

by Steve Mitchell
illustrations by
SCRAWLS

BANTAM BOOKS

THE COMPLETE HOW TO SPEAK SOUTHERN
A Bantam Book

PUBLISHING HISTORY
How to Speak Southern mass market edition / November 1976
More How to Speak Southern mass market edition / November 1980
The Complete How to Speak Southern hardcover edition / May 2006

Published by
Bantam Dell
A Division of Random House, Inc.
New York, New York

Book design by Glen M. Edelstein

Bantam Books is a registered trademark of Random House, Inc., and the
colophon is a trademark of Random House, Inc.

Library of Congress Cataloging-in-Publication Data

Mitchell, Steve.
The complete how to speak Southern / by Steve Mitchell ; with illustrations by
SCRAWLS (Sam C. Rawls).
p.   cm.
Combination of two books: How to speak Southern (1976) and
More how to speak Southern (1980).
ISBN-13: 978-0-553-80478-2
ISBN-10: 0-553-80478-2
1. English language—Southern States—Humor. 2. English language—Dialects—
Southern States—Glossaries, vocabularies, etc. I. Title: How to speak Southern.
II. Scrawls. III. Title.

PN6231.S64M58 2006
427'.9750207—dc22
2005057154

Printed in the United States of America
Published simultaneously in Canada

www.bantamdell.com

10   9   8   7   6   5   4
BVG

This book is dedicated to all Yankees
in the hope that it will
teach them how to talk right.

THE COMPLETE
HOW TO SPEAK SOUTHERN

A

ACit: That's it. "Ah (I) don't wanna hear no more about it. ACit as far as Ah'm concerned."

Addled: Confused, disoriented, as in the case of Northern sociologists who try to make sense out of the South. "What's wrong with that Yankee? He acts right addled."

AD-dress: Where you live. "What's your AD-dress, honey?"

A-DRESS: What women look very good in. "Jeans are nice, but I'd rather see a woman in a-DRESS."

Afar: In a state of combustion. "Call the far department. That house is afar."

Ah: The thing you see with, and the personal pronoun denoting individuality. "Ah think Ah've got somethin' in mah ah."

Ah 'magine: The first word means yourself—or as Southerners say, "yosef"—and the second is an expression of intent or belief. "Ah 'magine she's 'bout the sweetest gull (girl) in Jeff Davis County."

Ahce: Solidified liquid that is best employed in the cooling of mint juleps and aged bourbon. "This dry ink (drink) needs more ahce in it."

Ahdin: I didn't. "Ahdin know the gun was loaded, Judge."

Ahmoan: An expression of intent. "Ahmoan have a little drink. You want one?"

Ahms: What beggars ask for, but what Southern men hold their girls with. "Ah just want to put my ahms around you a little, is all."

Ahr: What we breathe, also a unit of time made up of 60 minutes. "They should've been here about an ahr ago."

Ahreen: A lady's name. "You remember that song that was popular during the Korean War? 'Goodnight Ahreen'?"

Aig: A breakfast food that may be fried, scrambled, boiled or poached. "Which came first, the chicken or the aig?"

Ails: 1. Else. "Warn't nothin', ma'am. Anybody ails would have done the same thing." 2. To be ill or afflicted by something. "That mule sure is actin' strange. Wonder what ails him?"

Aint: The sister of your mother or father. "Son, go over and give Aint Bea a big hug."

Airish: Drafty, cool. "Don't leave that door open. It's too airish already."

Airs: Mistakes. "That shortstop's made two airs, and the game's not half over yet."

All Ah wanna do is hold you a little, is all: One of the most brazen, outrageous lies Southern men tell women, and always with the utmost sincerity. "All Ah wanna do is hold you a little, is all, honey."

All over hell and half of Georgia: Covering a large area. "Ah've looked for that boy all over hell and half of Georgia."

AMbolance: A four-wheeled vehicle used to convey the injured to a hospital. "That boy's hurt bad. Better call an AMbolance."

Ar: Possessive pronoun. "That's ar dawg, not yours."

Argy: To dispute in a contentious manner. "Ah told you to take your bath, boy, and Ah'm not gonna stand here and argy with you about it."

AH SHOT AN ARRER INTO THE AHR... OWWW....

OLD ARN   NEW ARN

Arkensaw: A Southern state some Yankees have been known to confuse with Kansas, even though the two have nothing whatever to do with each other. "She's from Little Rock, Arkensaw."

Arn: An electrical instrument used to remove wrinkles from clothing. "Ah'm not gonna arn today. It's too hot."

Arrer: A pointed stick the Indians used to employ with great efficiency, as General George Custer discovered at Little Big Horn. "Ah shot an arrer into the ahr . . ."

Arshtaters: A staple of the Irish diet and the source of French fries. "Ah like arshtaters, but Ah hate to peel 'em."

Arthuritis: A painful illness characterized by stiffening of the joints and paralysis. "Grandma's arthuritis is botherin' her real bad today."

Ary: Not any. "He hadn't got ary cent."

Ast: To interrogate or inquire, as when a revenue agent seeks information about illegal moonshine stills. "Don't ast me so many questions. It makes me mad."

At: That. "Is at your car?"

Attair: Contraction used to indicate the specific item desired. "Pass me attair gravy, please."

Awduh: A state of affairs that depends on obedience to law. "The marshal brought law and awduh to this town."

Awf: The opposite of on. "Take your muddy feet awf the table."

Awficer: A policeman. "Well, Awficer, Ah guess Ah might have been goin' a little over the speed limit, but . . ."

Awfis: The place where men say they have to work late and sometimes actually do. "Go ahead and have supper without me, honey. Ah have to work late at the awfis."

Awfullest: The worst. "That's the awfullest lie you ever told me in your life."

Awl: An amber fluid used to lubricate engines. "Ah like that car, but it sure does use a lot of awl."

Awraht: Okay. "If you want to go back home to your mother, that's awraht with me."

AY-rab: The desert people who inhabit much of North Africa but not much of Israel. "That fella looks like a AY-rab, don't he?"

B

Babdist: A religious denomination whose members are found in great profusion throughout the South. They are against drinkin' and dancin', but . . . "Ah hear the Babdist preacher run off with the quar (choir) director."

Bad-mouth: To disparage or derogate. "All these candidates have bad-mouthed each other so much Ah've about decided not to vote for any of 'em."

Bad off: Desperately in need of, also extremely ill. 1. "Is that *Valley of the Dolls*? You must be bad off for somethin' to read." 2. "Jim's in the hospital. He's bad off."

Bad to: Inclined toward, prone to. "Johnny's bad to get in fights when he gets drunk."

Bait: A surfeit of. "Ah hope you get a bait of them spareribs, 'cause you've et about all of 'em."

Bard: To obtain the use of, not always on a temporary basis. "He bard mah shovel and never did bring it back."

Batry: A boxlike device that produces electricity. "Looks like your car's got a dead batry."

Bawl: What water does at 212 degrees Fahrenheit. "That gal cain't even bawl water without burnin' it."

Baws: Your employer. "The baws may not always be right, but he's always the baws."

Bawstun: The largest city in Massachusetts. "King George III didn't like the Bawstun Tea Party much."

Beholden: Indebted to. "Ah'm beholden to you for loanin' me that five dollars."

Best: Another baffling Southernism that is usually couched in the negative. "You best not speak to Cecil about his car. He just had to spend $300 on it."

Bidness: The art of selling something for more than you paid for it. "My cousin Archie is in the real estate bidness."

Bleeve: Expression of intent or faith. "Ah bleeve we ought to go to church this Sunday."

Bobbuh: One who cuts hair. "Ah wish you'd go to a different bobbuh."

Bobbycue: A delectable Southern sandwich that is prepared properly only in certain parts of North Carolina. It consists of chopped pork, cole slaw and a fiery sauce made chiefly of vinegar, red pepper and ketchup. "Four bobbycues to go, please."

Bobwar: A spiky strand of metal used to keep cattle inside an enclosed space. "Watch out, you'll get caught on that bobwar."

Body: Person, usually an oblique reference to yourself. "A body cain't get a minute's peace around this house."

Bound to: Certain to. "Too much beer is bound to give you a hangover."

Bounden determined: Totally committed to a course of action, not always the wisest. "She's bounden determined to marry him."

Bout: About, except in Tidewater, Virginia, where it is pronounced "aboot." "It's bout time to put out the far (fire) and call in the dawgs."

Bowut: In Charleston, South Carolina, a small craft that conveys one across water. "Where's the motor for this bowut?"

Boy: Any Southern white male under the age of 60, usually preceded by the words "good ole," meaning he

THET BOY AINT REAL BRAHT....

is amiable, likes a drink now and then and is fond of fishin', huntin' and good-lookin' women. "Clarence is a good ole boy."

Braht: 1. Dazzling."Venus is a braht planet."
2. Intelligence. "That Sue Ellen is the brahtest child in her class."

Branch: Part of a tree, but also what you use to cross a body of water. "We'll cross that branch when we come to it."

Break bad: To behave in a violent, wanton or outrageous manner for no discernible reason. "Ole Bill broke bad last night and wound up in jail."

Break of: To induce the abandonment of an undesirable trait or habit. "Ah'm gonna break that husband of mine of lyin' to me if it's the last thing Ah do."

Bub: A fragile glass object that converts electricity into illumination. "Ah think that light bub's burnt out."

Bud: Small feathered creature that flies. "A robin sure is a pretty bud."

Bum: An explosive device dropped from airplanes called bummers. "Ah think we ought to drop the atomic bum on 'em."

Bumminham: The biggest city in Alabama. "You can travel cross this entire land, they ain't no place like Bumminham."

C

Cain't: Cannot. "Ah just cain't understand why this checkbook won't balance."

Carry: To convey from one place to another, usually by automobile. "Can you carry me down to the store in yo' car?"

Cawse: Cause, usually preceded in the South by the adjective "lawst" (lost). "The War Between the States was a lawst cawse."

Cayut: A furry animal much beloved by little girls but detested by adults when it engages in mating rituals in the middle of the night. "Be sure to put the cayut outside before you go to bed."

Cent: The plural of *cent*. "You paid five dollars for that necktie? Ah wouldn't give fifty cent for it."

Chalstun: A city in South Carolina that Yankees call the Cradle of Secession. "Ah don't know why they're so upset. All we wanted was Fort Sumter back."

Cheer: A piece of furniture used for sitting. "Pull up a cheer and set a spell."

Chekatawlfarya?: An expression that is rapidly disappearing because of self-service gas stations, but one that still may be heard by baffled Yankees at service stations in small Southern towns. It translates as "Check that oil for you?"

Chimbley: What smoke comes out of. "Ah bleeve that chimbley's stopped up."

Chitlins: It is said that there are two things you should never see being made: laws and sausages. Chitlins are another. Chitlins, which can smell up the whole county when being cooked, are boiled and fried hog intestines. Delicious, if you can forget what they are. "Ah'll have another plate of them chitlins."

Chunk: To throw. "Chunk it in there, Leroy. Ole Leroy sure can chunk 'at ball, cain't he? Best pitcher we ever had."

Claws: An appendage to a legal document. "You'd be advised to study that claws very carefully."

Clawth: A woven material from which clothes are made. "Let me have three yards of that clawth, please."

Clone: A type of scent men put on themselves. "What's that clone you got on, honey?"

Co-cola: The soft drink that started in Atlanta and conquered the world. "Ah hear they even sell Co-cola in Russia."

Collards: A variety of kale, also known as greens. Southerners love them cooked with fatback, also known as the bacon that didn't quite make it. "Pass the collards, please."

CO-COLA

Collie flare: A crisp white vegetable that is surprisingly good once you get past the appearance. "Lots of boxers have collie flare ears."

Comin' up a cloud: An approaching storm. "Stay close to the house. It's comin' up a cloud."

COLLIE FLARE EAR

IT'S JUST A STANDARD CONTRACK. SIGN ON THE DOTTED LINE...

Commence to: To start or engage in some activity. "They got in a argyment, and the next thing you know, they commence to fight."

Commite nigh: To come very close to. "When Sue-Ann caught her husband kissin' that waitress from the Blue Moon, she commite nigh killin' him."

Contrack: A legal document, usually heavily in favor of the party who draws it up. "It's just a standard contrack . . . just sign right here."

Contrary: Obstinate, perverse. "Cecil's a fine boy, but she won't have nothin' to do with him. She's just contrary, is all Ah can figure."

Cooter: A large turtle found in Southern streams that supplemented many Dixie diets when the Yankees came down during Reconstruction and carried off everything that wasn't bolted down. "Goin' to the hardware store? Get me some cooter hooks."

Costes: The price of something. "Don't buy lettuce if it costes too much."

Cotta: One of our most beloved former presidents. "That Ol' President Cotta sure is sumpum, aint he?"

Crawss: The symbol of Christianity. "Ah love to hear 'em sing 'The Ole Rugged Crawss.' "

Crine: Weeping. "What's that girl crine about?"

Cuss: Profane language, or a malediction. "The Hope Diamond has got a cuss on it."

Cut awf: To switch off. "It's too bright in here, honey. Why don't we cut awf that light bub?"

Cut the fool: To behave in a silly or foolish manner. "Quit cuttin' the fool and do your homework."

Cyst: To render aid. "Can Ah cyst you with those packages, ma'am?"

D

Daints: A more or less formal event in which members of the opposite sex hold each other and move rhythmically to the sound of music. "You wanna go to the daints with me Saturday night, Wilma Sue?"

Damyankee: Anyone who is not from one of the eleven Confederate states. "Ah was ten years old before Ah found out damyankee was two words."

Danjuh: Imminent peril. What John Paul Jones meant when he said, "Give me a fast ship, for I intend to put her in harm's way."

Darest: Old English contraction of dare not, meaning unadvisable to. "You darest talk about the stock market around your daddy since he lost all that money in it."

Dawfins: Name of the professional football team in Miami. "You think the Dawfins can win the conference this year?"

Dawg: A four-legged animal much esteemed in rural sections of the South. "Ah just don't feel right unless Ah got a couple of huntin' dawgs around the house."

Dayum: A cuss word Rhett Butler used in *Gone With the Wind.* "Frankly, my deah, Ah don't give a dayum."

Deah: 1. A term of endearment. 2. A four-legged animal with antlers. "Floyd wouldn't dream of missin' openin' day of deah season."

OOooo, CLARK, WHAT YOU JUST SAID!

Deppity: A county law enforcement officer. "Bob's a deppity shurf."

Dewk: A prestigious university in North Carolina with an excellent basketball team. "Dewk could go all the way this year."

Dewty: Something that must be done even when it is difficult. "Robert E. Lee said dewty was the most sublime word in the English language."

Didn't go to: Did not intend to. "Don't whip Billy for knockin' his little sister down. He didn't go to do it."

Dinner: The meal Southerners eat while Northerners are eating lunch. When the Northerners are eating dinner, Southerners are eating supper. "We're just

HONEY... AH THINK IT'S ABOUT TIME YOU WENT ON A DITE...

havin' butterbeans and biscuits for dinner, but we'll have a big supper."

Dite: What people do to lose weight. "Honey, Ah think it's about time you went on a dite."

Doc: A condition caused by an absence of light. "It's mighty doc in here."

Dollin: Another term of endearment. Southern men call almost ALL women darling, even those they have met only a few minutes before. "You call EVERYBODY dollin."

Done: 1. Finished. "Are you done eatin'?" 2. Already. "Has the bus done gone?"

Don't differ: Makes no difference. "It don't differ to me whether we go or not."

Down in: Afflicted with spinal pain. "Ole Jim's down in his back."

Draff: A current of chilling air, or Selective Service, which is much the same thing in the minds of many young people today. "Ah got a solution to the problem of teenage unrest. Bring back the draff."

Drank: To consume a liquid. "You want a drank of this Co-cola?"

Draw up: To contract or shrink. "Ah told you that blouse would draw up if you washed it in hot water."

Dreckly: Soon. "He'll be along dreckly."

Drinkin' liquor: Exceptionally smooth whiskey. "Ah don't want no fightin' liquor. Gimme a bottle of your best drinkin' liquor."

Duck: Conduit or pipe. "Hand me that roll of duck tape."

Duddinit: Doesn't it. "Duddinit feel sort of cool in here?"

Dun: To send a bill for money owed. "That finance company's about to dun me to death."

E

Earl: A metal device used to improve radio and television reception. "You could pick up a lot more stations if you had a higher TV earl."

Eat up with: Excessively afflicted by. "That woman's jest eat up with jealousy."

Effuts: Exertions. "Lee made great effuts to defeat Grant, but that's hard to do when you're outnumbered three to one."

Et: To have eaten. "You done et?"

Etlanna: The city General Sherman burned during the War for Southern Independence. "Etlanna is kind of like New York with pecan trees."

Everhoo: Another baffling Southernism—a reverse contraction of whoever. "Everhoo one of you kids wants to go to the movie better clean up their room."

Everthang: All-encompassing. "Everthang's all messed up."

Everwhichaways: To be scattered in all directions. "You should have been there when the train hit that chicken truck. Them chickens flew everwhichaways."

Eyetalyun: A native of Italy or an American ethnic group of that heritage. "You don't have to be Eyetalyun to like spaghetti."

MAMA MIA, YOU DON'TA HAVE TO BE EYETALYUN TO ENJOYA SPAGHET, YAWL.

FARN LIQUOR
F

Fa: A long distance. "Don't git too fa from the house."

Fahn: Excellent. "That sure is a fahn-lookin' woman."

Fair off: A Southern weather report, usually delivered by a laconic mountaineer who claims Indian blood and expertise in such matters. "It's stopped rainin'. Looks like it's gonna fair off."

Far: A state of combustion that produces heat and light. "Ah reckon it's about time to put out the far and call in the dawgs."

Farn: Anything that is not domestic. "Ah don't drink no farn liquor, specially Rooshin vodka."

Fatback: Salt pork—an essential ingredient in the cooking of collard greens and beans. "Ah like fried-out fatback as much as bacon."

Fatnen hawg: Descriptive term applied to the obese. "Put on weight? He's like a fatnen hawg."

Fault: To place blame. "You can't fault a man for takin' a little drank of liquor once in a while."

Favor: To resemble. "That boy sure does favor his daddy, don't he?"

Fawl: What happens when you lose your balance. "He tripped over the cayut and took a bad fawl."

Fawn: The instrument a drunken ex-Army buddy uses to call you long distance in the middle of the night to reminisce about old times. "Honey, would you get up and answer the fawn? If it's Billy Bob from Texas, tell him we got divorced and Ah moved up to Alaska."

Fawt: What Yankees and Southerners did when the South asked for a divorce back in 1861 and the North refused to grant it. "Nobody fawt like Stonewall Jackson."

Fawud: Straight ahead, which is the direction General Lee preferred to take. "Fawud, ho!"

Fayan: An electrical appliance that circulates air. "It's hot in here. Cut own that fayan."

Fell off: To have lost weight. "She's not near as fat as she used to be. That girl's fell off a lot."

Fem: A necessary ingredient in the creation of photographs. "Are you sure you got fem in that camera?"

Fetchin': Attractive. "That's a mighty fetchin' woman. Think Ah'll ask her to daints."

Fixin': Preparing to. "Ah'm fixin' to dig me some worms and go fishin'."

Fizu: Abbreviated version of "If I were you." "Fizu, Ah'd get outta here."

Fladuh: The Sunshine State. "Two things we like to pick in Fladuh are oranges and tourists."

Flares: The colorful, sweet-smelling part of a plant. "If yo wife's mad at you, it's smart to take her some flares."

SAY IT WITH FLARES

Flat out: A Southern stock car racing expression, meaning put the pedal on the metal and see how fast she'll go. "Junior Johnson didn't know but one way to drive—flat out."

Fline: To travel by air. "Ah like fline, but why do they make the seats so little and jam 'em so close together?"

Foller: Spies and private detectives spend a lot of time doing this. "Quick . . . Get a cab! We got to foller that car!"

Foolin' around: Can mean not doing anything in particular, or sex, usually of the extramarital variety.

"Suellen caught her husband foolin' around, so she divorced him."

Fore: Goffers (golfers) holler it before they hit the little white ball, but it also means "prior to" in the South. "This was a nice party fore they got here."

Frawg: A greenish amphibian whose legs are much esteemed by diners. "Ah'll have an order of frawg legs, miss."

Fummeer: A place other than one's present location. "Where do we go fummeer?"

Fur piece: A considerable distance. "It's a fur piece from here to Jacksonville."

G

Garntee: Any sort of warranty, frequently honored more in the breach than in the observance. "The store said the garntee didn't cover that."

Gawn: Departed. "Debby Lee's not here. She's gawn out with somebody else."

Git: To acquire. "If you're goin' to the store, git me a six-pack of beer."

Git by with: To get away with. "You think yo wife's gonna bleeve that story? You'll never git by with it."

Git own: To expedite matters. "Let's git own with it."

Git shed of: To rid oneself of. "That car is costin' me too much money, and Ah'm gonna git shed of it."

Give up to be: Generally conceded to be. "He's give up to be the crookedest lawyer in the whole state of Mississippi."

Go to: Intend. "You shouldn't have whipped Jimmy for breakin' that window. He didn't go to do it."

Go to the bad: To spoil. "Put that mayonnaise back in the refrigerator or it'll go to the bad."

Goff: A game played with clubs and a little white ball, usually to the accompaniment of much profanity. "Ah hate goff."

Gone: Going to. "You boys just git out there and play football. We gone make mistakes, but they are, too."

Goobers: Peanuts. "It's fun to put goobers in a Co-cola and watch it foam."

Good ole boy: Any Southern male between the ages of 16 and 60 who has an amiable disposition and is fond of boon companions, strong drink, hound dawgs, fishin', huntin' and good-lookin' women, but not necessarily in that order. "Basil's a good ole boy."

Got a good notion: A statement of intent. "Ah got a good notion to cut a switch and whale the dickens out of that boy."

Got in the wind of: To discover. "Purvis was foolin' around with some topless dancer 'til his wife got in the wind of it and went upside his head with a fryin' pan."

"JEST A GOOD OLE BOY"

Gracious plenty: Enough or more than enough. "Don't let me eat any more of that country ham. I've had a gracious plenty."

Grain of sense: An appraisal of intelligence, invariably expressed in negative terms. "That boy ain't got a grain of sense."

Grammaw: The Southern matriarch, both black and white, who is the absolute dictator of most Southern families: the grandmother. "You better run home. Grammaw's callin'."

Grampaw: Her male counterpart. "Grampaw's the head of the house 'cause Grammaw lets him think he is."

GRAMMAW GRAMPAW

Griyuts: What no Southern breakfast would be complete without—grits. "Ah like griyuts with butter and sawt on 'em, but Ah purely love 'em with red-eye gravy."

Guff: An oil company. "Where's the high school? Well, you go down this road for two blocks and turn left at the Guff station . . ."

Gull: A female. "She's just about the sweetest, prettiest gull in town."

Gummut: A large institution operating out of Washington that consumes taxes at a fearful rate. "Bill's got it made. He's got a gummut job."

H

Hah: High. "Yeah, you can climb that tree, son. Just don't get up too hah."

Hahr: That which grows on your head and requires cutting periodically. "You need a hahrcut."

Haint: A ghost, spirit or apparition. "If you walk past the graveyard at midnight, you might see a haint."

Haired: A man's first name. "Ah miss *Monday Night Football* with Haired Cosell."

Hale: Where General Sherman is going for what he did to Etlanna. "General Sherman said, 'War is hale,' and he made sure it was."

Hard: To secure employment. "Ah didn't get that job. They hard somebody else."

Hawg: A noble and eminently edible animal which furnishes Southerners with such delicacies as country ham, spareribs, fatback, fried pork skins, pickled pig's feet and chopped pork for barbecue. "When it gits to be cold weather, you know it's time to kill hawgs."

Hawnky-tawnk: A Southern bar or tavern, also known as a jook joint. "Don't you stay out all night at some hawnky-tawnk."

Heepa: A great deal of. "You in a heepa trouble, boy."

Hep: To aid or benefit. "Ah cain't hep it if Ah'm still in love with you."

Hern (and Hisn): Feminine possessive and the opposite of hisn. "Is that blonde hair really hern?"

Hit a lick at a snake: Lazy, or as Southerners say, sorry. "He's too sorry to hit a lick at a snake."

Hod: Not soft, but meaning stubborn or willful when used to describe a Southern child's head. "That boy's so hod-headed it's pitiful."

Honey: A universal term of address when speaking to female children in the South. "Honey, come here and give Grammaw a big kiss."

Hot: A muscle that pumps blood through the body, but also regarded as the center of emotion. "That gull (girl) has just about broke his hot."

Husbun: The male half of a madge (marriage). "He's her second husbun."

Hush yo' mouth: An expression of pleased embarrassment, as when a Southern female is paid an extravagant compliment. "Honey, you're 'bout the sweetest, best-lookin' woman in Tennessee." "Now, hush yo' mouth, Bobby Lee Jackson."

Hyuh: Word used to summon dawgs. "Hyuh, boy, hyuh!"

BROKEN HOT

I

Idinit: Term employed by genteel Southerners who wish to avoid saying "Ain't." "Mighty hot today, idinit?"

Idy: Idea. "Have you got any idy the tricks that dawg can do?"

If you cain't listen, you can feel: What errant Southern children are told just prior to a World Class whipping. "Ah told you to leave that cat alone. If you cain't listen, you can feel!"

Ignert: Ignorant. "Ah've figgered out what's wrong with Congress. Most of 'em are just plain ignert."

Ill: Angry, testy. "What's wrong with Mavis today? She's ill as a hornet."

In a manner: A baffling redundancy sometimes inserted into a sentence. "That baby acts like it's starvin' in a manner to death," meaning the baby appears hungry.

IN-shurnce: A system in which you stand to come into a great deal of money when you die. "Ah'm with the Octopus IN-shurnce Comp'ny. Would it be convenient for me to stop by and talk with you this evenin'?"

Innerduce: To make one person acquainted with another. "Lemme innerduce you to my cousin. She's a little on the heavy side, but she's got a great personality."

Iont: I don't. "Iont know if I can eat another bobbycue (barbecue) or not."

Izril: A nation of which Southerners are inordinately fond, mainly because they respect its fighting ability. "You 'member what Izril done in the Six Day War?"

J

Jack-leg: Self-taught, especially in reference to automobile mechanics and clergymen. "He's just a jack-leg preacher, but he sure knows how to put out the hellfire and brimstone."

Jawja: Southern state just north of Florida. "Sherman burnt Etlanna when he marched through Jawja."

Jevver: Did you ever. "Jevver hear anything so dumb in your life?"

Jew: Did you. "Jew want to buy that comic book, son, or just stand there and read it here?"

Jewant: Do you want. "Jewant to go over to the Red Rooster and have a few beers?"

Jookin': To visit a variety of Southern nightspots, many of which are frequented by gentlemen who are armed and dangerous. Jookin' mainly involves drinkin', dancin' and, sometimes, fightin'. "Why don't we go jookin' tonight, honey?"

K

Ka-yun: A sealed cylinder containing food. "If that woman didn't have a kay-un opener, her family would starve to death."

Keer: To be concerned. "That girl don't keer nothin' about him."

Kep: Kept. "Ah kep tellin' you not to do that."

Kerosene cat in hell with gasoline drawers on: A colorful Southern expression used as an evaluation of someone's ability to accomplish something. "He ain't got no more chance than a kerosene cat in hell with gasoline drawers on."

Kin: Related to. An Elizabethan expression, one of many which survive in the South. "Are you kin to him?" "Yeah. He's my brother."

Kindly: Sort of. "When Ed's line broke and he lost that big bass, he just looked kindly pale and sick."

Klect: To receive money to which one is entitled. "Ah don't think you'll ever klect that bill."

Kumpny: Guests. "Be home on time. We're havin' kumpny for supper."

LAHTNIN' BUG

L

Lahf: The opposite of death. "Nobody said lahf was going to be easy."

Laht: 1. The opposite of dark. "This room's too doc (dark). We need more laht in here." 2. Also a source of illumination, as in the immortal Hank Williams's rendition of "Ah Saw the Laht."

Lahtnin' bug: A firefly. "You don't see many lahtnin' bugs anymore. Wonder why?"

Lam: Sheep, which most Southerners regard with the deepest possible suspicion as a source of food. "Ah ain't eatin' NOTHIN' that smells like Wildroot Cream Oil, and that's what lam smells like to me."

Lanyop: Lagniappe. In Louisiana, a little something extra. "Ah bought a dozen doughnuts, and he threw in another one as lanyop."

Lar: One who tells untruths. "Not all fishermen are lars. It's just that a lot of lars fish."

Law: Police, or as Southerners pronounce it, PO-leece. "We better get out of here. That bartender's done called the law."

Lawg: Part of a tree trunk. "It's phrasin (freezin') in here. Put another lawg on the far."

Lawst: To be unsure of one's location. "This road don't go nowhere. We're lawst."

Layin' up: Resting or meditating. Or as Southern women usually put it, loafing. "Cecil didn't go to work today 'cause of a chronic case of laziness. He's been layin' up in the house all day, drivin' me crazy."

Learn: Teach. "Ah'm gonna take a two-by-four to that mule and learn him some sense."

Least one: Smallest. Generally used in reference to children. "Johnny's my oldest, and Sue Ann is the least one."

Lectricty: A mysterious force that gives us heat, illumination, television and all sorts of wondrous things while bringing great profit to the pare (power) companies. "You cain't see lectricty, but it's there."

Lekshun: A political contest. "Who you think's gonna win the lekshun?"

Let alone: Much less. "He cain't even hold a job and support himself, let alone support a family."

Let on: To indicate knowledge of, either by word or action. "Her husband's been drunk for ten years, but don't let on you know anything about it."

Libel: Likely to. "If your wife finds out you're runnin' around with that go-go dancer, she's libel to kill you."

... AND WIF YO HEP...I KIN WIN THIS LEKSHUN.

Lick: A blow. "You and Billy got in a fight? Who passed the first lick?"

Lick and a promise: To do something in a hurried or perfunctory fashion. "We don't have time to clean this house so it's spotless. Just give it a lick and a promise."

LIE-berry: A building containing thousands upon thousands of literary works. "This book's overdue at the LIE-berry."

Light bread: A pre-sliced loaf of soft, store-bought bread that no Southern woman would have dared to place before her family in older and simpler times. "Git this light bread off the table, woman, and fix me some hot biscuits."

Like to: Almost. "When Ah saw she had on the same dress Ah did, Ah like to died."

LIGHT BREAD

BISCUIT   CORN BREAD

(REAL BREAD)

Likker: Whiskey; either the amber kind bought in stores or the homemade white kind the federal authorities frown upon. "Does he drink? Listen, he spills more likker than most people drink."

Lil: Small. "That lil ole puppy sure is cute, ain't he?"

Lowance: A weekly sum of money paid to children in the hope of inducing reasonably good behavior. "Unless you clean up your room, you won't git your lowance this week."

M

Ma'am (and Suh): Archaic terms of courtesy and
respect Southern children once were taught to use
when addressing their elders. "Now, when you talk to
your teacher, you make sure you say 'Yes, ma'am' and
'No, ma'am,' you hear me?"

Madge: A state of wedlock that any preacher can put
you into, but only a lawyer can get you out of. "Seems
like a lot of madges end in divorce these days."

Mah: Possessive personal pronoun. "Anybody seen
mah huntin' boots?"

Mahty raht: Correct. "You mahty raht about that,
Awficer. Guess Ah WAS speedin' a little bit."

Make out: Yes, it means that in the South, too, but it
also means finish your meal. "You chirren (children)
hav'n't had nearly enough to eat. Make out your
supper."

Mash: To press, as in the case of an elevator button. "Want me to mash yo floor for you, ma'am?"

Mast: A disguise over part of the face. "Who was that mast man?" "Why, that was the Lone Ranger."

Maul: A shopping center. "You been out to the new maul?"

Mawk: Mock; to make fun of, usually by imitating accents or mannerisms. "You ought to hear him mawk the President."

Mere: A reflective glass. "Mere, mere, on the wall, who's the fairest of them all?"

Mess: A quantity of, usually enough for a meal. "That's a nice mess of fish."

Mind: To obey. "Now, you mind yo big sister while Ah'm at the store, you hear?"

Mind to: To have the intention of doing something. "Ah got a mind to quit my job and just loaf for a while."

Mite could: Might possibly. "If you'd invest in real estate you mite could make a lot of money."

Miz: Southern form of address stolen by the Women's Liberation movement. "Is that Miz Thompson comin' down the street?"

Moanin': Between daybreak and noon. "Good moanin', suh."

Mommocked up: Damaged or defaced. "Don't try to paint the table with that old stiff brush. You'll jest get it mommocked up."

Moon pah: A round, chocolate-covered cake with a marshmallow filling that is traditionally consumed with a Royal Crown Cola, which Southerners refer to as an ArCee. "Let's have a ArCee and a moon pah."

MOON PAH

ARCEE

Motuhsickle: A two-wheeled missile with a powerful engine that is capable of great speed and is inherently unstable, thus providing physicians, hospitals and funeral directors with a regular source of income. "Johnny had his motuhsickle up to 120 last night."

Muchablige: Thank you. "Muchablige for the lift, mister."

Munts: The 12 units into which the calendar year is divided. "Ah hadn't seen Bob in about three munts."

N

Nachur: Nature, but in the sense of sex drive or libido. "When you have a tom cat neutered, it takes away his nachur."

Naht: The opposite of day. "You might say Dracula was a naht person."

Nairn: Not any; not a one. "Ah'd offer you a cigarette, but Ah don't have nairn."

Nawth: Any part of the country outside the South— Midwest, California or whatever. If it's not South, it's Nawth. "People from up Nawth sure do talk funny."

Nawthun: Anything that is not Southern. "He is a classic product of the superior Nawthun educational system." (Sarcasm)

Nekkid: To be unclothed. "Did you see her in that new movie? She was nekkid as a jaybird."

Nemmine: Never mind, but used in the sense of difference. "It don't make no nemmine to me."

Nome: A child's negative reply to a female adult's question. "Jimmy, did you pull that cat's tail?" "Nome."

Nooclar: Having to do with atomic power. "Jake's got a good job over at the nooclar plant."

Not about to: To have no intention of. "Ah'm not about to pay $50,000 for a new car."

Nyawlins: The largest city in Louisiana (pronounced Loosyana). "Nyawlins is a nice town if you got a lot of money."

O

Oakree: A ridged, elongated vegetable, known to the few Yankees who know about it as okra. "Ah don't like oakree any way but fried in flour with corn bread."

Of a moanin': Of a morning, meaning in the morning. "My daddy always liked his coffee of a moanin'."

Orta: Should. "You orta see her in that bikini."

Ose: A type of car produced by General Motors. "That '55 Ose was the best car Ah ever had."

Ovair: In that direction. "Where's yo daddy, son?" "He's ovair, suh."

Own: Opposite of awf. "Cut own the radio and let's listen to some music."

Ownliest: The only one. "That's the ownliest one Ah've got left."

PART MAKING AIR

P

Pal: Powell. "Colin Pal was a good general."

Pannyhos: A misbegotten hybrid of stocking and girdle foisted off on Southern (and American) womanhood by malevolent clothing designers bent on wiping out heterosexuality. "Ah hate pannyhos."

Papuh: What you write on; also, the colloquial term for newspaper. "Which papuh do you take?"

Pare: Strength, authority. "Never underestimate the pare of a woman."

Parts: Buccaneers who sailed under the dreaded skull and crossbones. "See that third baseman? He just signed a big contrack with the Pittsburgh Parts."

NEVER UNDERESTIMATE THE PARE OF A WOMAN

Passel: A large quantity. "Ah'm cookin' up a passel of collard greens for supper."

Pattun: A diagram to follow when making clothing. "Ah've got the nicest pattun for a new Easter dress."

Pawl: A man's name. "My momma said Pawl was the cutest Beatle."

PEE-cans: Northerners call them pe-CONNS for some obscure reason, but they are thin-shelled nuts that translate themselves wonderfully into the Southern delicacy called PEE-can pie. "Honey, go out in the yard and pick up a passel of PEE-cans. Ah'm gonna make us a pie."

Penny one: None at all, nothing. "He's been owin' me five dollars for five years, and Ah have yet to see penny one of it."

Pentoes: Reddish-brown beans that constitute a staple of Southern diet because they get better every time they're reheated. "Ah druther have hot biscuits and a big plate of pentoes than steak."

Peppuh: A hot spice widely used to season food. "Pass the peppuh, please."

Pert: Perky, full of energy. "You look mighty pert today."

Peyun: A writing instrument. "Some rob you with a six-gun, and some with a fountain peyun."

Phrasin': Very cold. "Shut that door. It's phrasin' in here."

Picayunish: Overly fastidious, picky. "That little blood spot won't hurt that egg. Don't be so picayunish."

Pick at: To pester and annoy. "Jimmy, Ah told you not to pick at your little sister. If you cain't listen, you can feel."

Picked up: To have gained weight. "You've picked up a little, haven't you?"

Pinny: One hundredth part of a dollar and so valueless these days that most people don't even pick them up when they drop them. "Ah don't owe him a pinny."

Pitcher: An image, either drawn or photographed. "That's a good pitcher of Brenda Sue."

Play like: To pretend. "You play like you're the nurse and Ah'll be the doctor."

Plum: Completely. "Ah'm plum wore out."

Poke: A brown paper bag. "What's in that poke—lunch or likker?"

PO-leece: One or more law enforcement officers. "Ah was jest standin' there mindin' my own bidness, Judge, when this here PO-leece come up to me . . ."

Pore: 1. Destitute. "They're as pore as church mice." 2. Inferior or second-rate. "A pore excuse is better than none."

Pot likker: The rich liquid left in the pot after the greens have been cooked for several hours. May be drunk or sopped up with biscuits. "Pot likker is full of vitamins and minerals."

Prolly: Likely to. "Ah'll prolly go to Etlanna this weekend."

Pup: What they turn trees into to make papuh. "Ah'm gonna beat him to a pup."

Pupwood: A soft wood used in the manufacture of papuh. "He's got about a thousand acres of good pupwood to sell."

Purtiest: The most pretty. "Ain't she the purtiest thing you ever seen?"

Q

Quar: An organized choral group, usually connected with a church or school. "Did you hear the news? The preacher left his wife and run off with the quar director."

Quare: Strange, peculiar. "Ole Virgil's been actin' quare ever since that mule kicked him in the head."

Quietus: Pronounced kwi-EET-us and meaning to bring to an abrupt halt. "He was runnin' around with that blonde waitress from the Blue Moon Cafe 'til his wife found out about it and put the quietus on it."

R

Raffle: A long-barreled firearm. "Dan'l Boone was a good shot with a raffle."

Rahtnaow: At once. "Linda Sue, Ah want you to tell that boy it's time to go home and come in the house rahtnaow."

Rahts: Rights. "When I asked those Johnny Reb prisoners what they were fighting for, I thought they said they were fighting for their rahts."

WHOOEEE... THAT'S SOME RAFFLE!

Ranch: A tool used to loosen or tighten nuts and bolts. "Hand me that ranch, Homer."

Rare back: What a horse does just prior to throwing you off the saddle. "When you see a cobra rare back, you know he's gettin' ready to strike."

Ratcheer: On this spot. "Jest put the groceries down ratcheer."

Raut: A method of getting from one place to another, which Southerners pronounce to rhyme with "kraut." Yankees, for reasons that remain shrouded in mystery, pronounce "route" to rhyme with "root." Or worse still, "foot."

Rawsin: The sap that oozes from pine trees. "Fiddlers put rawsin on their bows."

Reckon: An expression of supposition or intent. "Where do you reckon he got that plaid suit?"

Reckonize: The realization of seeing something familiar. "Why, you're the fella that plays the Lone Ranger on TV. Ah didn't reckonize you without your mast (mask)."

Recud: Round pieces of plastic that emit music when played on a stereo. "That's a nice recud. Play it again."

Redbugs: Chiggers. "Put some insek (insect) spray on your legs so you don't get redbugs."

Rench: To wash off soapy water with clear water. "Ah'll wash the dishes if you'll rench 'em."

Rernt: Ruined. "That boy's drove that car so rough he's plum rernt it."

Rester: To be accounted for by the government. "You kids today are lucky. When Ah was your age, Ah had to rester for the draff. They almost got me, too."

Restrunt: A place to eat. "New York's got a lot of good restrunts."

Retard: No longer employed. "He's retard now."

Retch: To grasp for. "The right fielder retch over into the stands and caught the ball."

Richmun: The capital of the Confederacy that exists today only because General Sherman ran out of matches. "He's hanging around that girl like Grant hung around Richmun."

Right smart: A goodly amount. "She's put on a right smart of weight lately."

Robut E. Lee: The finest gentleman who ever drew breath and the greatest military leader since Julius Caesar and Alexander the Great. "Robut E. Lee didn't surrender. Grant just stole his sword and Lee

ROBUT E. LEE: THE FINEST GENTLEMAN WHO EVER DREW BREATH...

was too much of a gentleman to ast him to give it back."

Rostenears: Fresh corn suitable for roasting or boiling. "Go over to the cornfield and pick me a dozen nice rostenears."

Ruut: The underground part of a tree which Southerners rightly pronounce to rhyme with "toot." Yankees pronounce it to rhyme with "foot." Nobody knows why.

S

Saar: The opposite of sweet. "These pickles are too saar."

Sandy Claws: The fat jolly man who comes down the chimbley every Christmas. "Did Sandy Claws bring you a lot of presents?"

Sass: Another Elizabethan term derived from the word *saucy*, meaning to speak in an impertinent manner. "Don't sass me, young lady. You're not too old to get a whuppin'."

Sawt: The ocean is full of it, and so is country ham. "Lot's wife looked back at Sodom and Gomorrah and turned into a pillar of sawt."

Sayul: Sale. Some radio announcers, in a misguided attempt to sound sophisticated, pronounce it to rhyme with "sell": "Don't miss the big sayul."

Scapped: An unpleasant operation formerly carried out by Indians. "That bobbuh (barber) scapped you."

Scupter: One who makes statues out of rock. "Michelangelo was a good scupter."

Scuse: To beg someone's pardon. "Scuse me, ma'am."

Sebmlebm: A convenience store. "Stop by the Sebmlebm and get me a six-pack of beer."

Sebmty: A ripe old age—seven decades, to be exact. "He's sebmty years old."

Sebmup: Soft drink similar to ginger ale. "You want a Co-cola or a Sebmup?"

SEE-ment: A mixture that turns into concrete. "Be careful and don't step on that wet SEE-ment."

SEM-eye: Partially. "Did you see that movie 'SEM-eye Tough'?"

Set: Sit. "Come on in and set a spell."

Shainteer: Indicates the absence of a female. "Is the lady of the house in?" "Nope. Shainteer."

Shalot: The biggest city in Nawth Calina. "People who live in Shalot are called Shalotteans."

Share: To cleanse oneself with water. "Why does somebody always call up when Ah'm takin' a share?"

Shawt: The opposite of long. "She likes Willie, but she thinks he's too shawt for her."

Shovelay: A General Motors car. "Nobody could drive a Shovelay like Junior Johnson."

Show: Certainly. "It show is hot today."

Shudenoughta: Should not. "You shudenoughta have another drink."

Shuhmun: The Yankee general, William Tecumseh, who said "War is hale" and proved it. "Shuhmun burned Etlanna (Atlanta)."

Shurf: A county's chief law enforcement officer. "The shurf's raidin' bootleg joints again. Must be a lekshun year."

Sinner: The exact middle of. "Have you been out to that new shoppin' sinner?"

Skase: Hard to find; in very short supply. "During the waw [war], sugar was skase."

Skawld: To burn with hot water. "You have to skawld a hawg after you kill it."

CAREFUL... ...DON'T SKAWLD YERSELF...

Slip off: To absent oneself, usually by stealth. "Where'd that boy slip off to? He was right here a minute ago."

Smore: An additional amount. "Want smore corn bread?"

Sorry: Lazy, shiftless. "That woman's so sorry she won't even make hot biscuits."

Spaded: To render a female animal incapable of producing offspring. "You ought to have that cat spaded before she has any more kittens."

Speakuh: One who speaks. "Who's the Speakuh of the House?"

Spear: The opposite of inferior. "Ah couldn't get no satisfaction from that clerk, so Ah asked to see her immediate spear."

Spearmint: Something scientists do. "Dr. Frankenstein decided to do this spearmint, see, and he ended up with a monster."

Spect: To imagine or suppose. "Ah spect a girl as sweet and pretty as she is could have 'bout any man she wanted."

Spell: An indeterminate length of time. "Let's set here and rest a spell."

Spittin' image: Southern pronunciation of "spirit and image," meaning similarity of appearance. "She's the spittin' image of her mother."

Spose: Suppose. "Spose you and me was to get married?"

Squeezins: What they make in stills—a volatile derivative of corn also known as moonshine, shine and white liquor. "Ah wouldn't mind havin' a little drink of squeezins about now."

Srimp: A small crustacean much beloved by residents of the Guff (Gulf) Coast. "They sure love srimp and crawfish in Loosyana."

Stain: The opposite of leaving. "Ah hate this party, and Ah'm not stain much longer."

Standin' in need of: Another redundancy thrown in for no other reason than Southerners love rolling rhetoric and extravagant language. It simply means to need or want. "Ah'm standin' in need of a cold beer."

Steal: What they make moonshine in. "The revenoors found pappy's steal."

Story: The polite euphemism for an untruth. "She said she was stain home tonight. That girl told me a story!"

Stow: Place where things are sold. "Son, Ah want you to go to the stow and get me some bakin' powder."

Studyin': Having an interest in, usually expressed negatively. "She said Ah wanted to date Homer? Ah'm not studyin' that boy."

Subject to: Inclined in the direction of; prone to. "Tom's a good ole boy, but he's subject to get drunk every now and then."

Sugar: A kiss. "Come here and give your momma some sugar."

Summers: Somewhere. "Ah know that boy's around here summers."

Sumpm: Something. "There's sumpm funny goin' on."

Supper: The evening meal Southerners are having while Yankees are having dinner. "What's for supper, honey?"

YANKEE
SUGAR

SOUTHERN
SUGAR

Suthun: The opposite of Nawthun. "Black-eyed peas and collard greens are Suthun dishes."

Swaller: To transfer from the mouth to the stomach. "My throat's so sore Ah cain't hardly swaller."

Swayge down: The process of a swollen area returning to normal, derived from the Old English *assuage*. "If you lance a boil, it'll swayge down."

Swimmy-headed: Dizzy. "Don't drink that ice water so fast. It'll make you swimmy-headed."

Switch: Slender branch of a tree employed in the behavior modification of children. "Ah'm gonna cut me a switch and wear that boy out."

T

Tacky: An expression used by Southern females and almost always in regard to wearing apparel. Can mean anything from unfashionable to downright ugly. "Did you see that dress she was wearin'? Honey, it was so tacky. . . ."

Tah: A useless appurtenance men feel compelled to wear around their necks. "Ah hate to wear a tah."

Tahm: A Yankee dictionary defines it as "A nonspatial continuum in which events occur in apparently irreversible succession from the past through the present to the future." Let's just say you either have too much of it or not enough. "It takes a long tahm to read the Sunday New York *Tahms*."

Take on: To behave in a highly emotional manner. "Don't take on like that, Brenda Sue. He's not the only man in Lee County."

Taken: Took. "You won't go wrong on that blue Ford. Ah taken it in trade off a Sunday School teacher. Don't use a drop of oil."

Tal: What you dry off with after you take a share. "Would you bring me a tal, sweethcart?"

Tamarr: The day after today. "Tamarr's a school day."

Tapern: To narrow to a point. "W.C. don't drink near as much as he used to. He's tapern off."

Tar: A round inflatable object that sometimes goes flat. "You shouldn't drive that car without a spare tar."

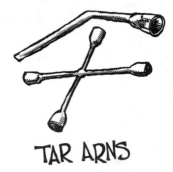

TAR ARNS

Tar arn: Tool employed in changing wheels. "You cain't change a tar without a tar arn."

Tare: 1. To rip. 2. A high building. "Over in Italy, we saw the Leanin' Tare of Pizza."

Tarred: Fatigued. "Ah'm too tarred to go bowlin' tonight."

Tawk: A method of communication that still flourishes in the South in spite of television. "How come people from up Nawth say we tawk funny when they're the ones who tawk funny?"

Tawt: To instruct. "Don't pull that cat's tail. Ah tawt you better'n that."

Tewsdee: The day before Wednesday. "If this is Mondee, tamarr must be Tewsdee."

Teyun: The number that comes after nine. "He's broke all the Teyun Commandments but one, and that's just 'cause he couldn't figure out how to make graven images."

Thang: A word Yankees consistently mispronounce as "Theeng." "Have you seen Sue Ann's new boyfriend? Honey, he's just the cutest thang."

Thank: Think. "Ah thank Ah'll go to a movie tonight."

Tharties: Authorities, usually police and prosecutors. "Don't take that money, Congressman. It could be from the tharties."

That dawg won't hunt: That will not work. "You want to borrow twenty dollars when you still owe me fifty? That dawg won't hunt."

Thawt: The process of thinking. "He's lawst in thawt."

They: There. "They ain't no use tryin' to fight City Hall."

Thoo: Finished, completed. "Ah'm bout thoo with this book."

Thow: To hurl. "Quick, thow me the ball!"

Throw off on: To cast aspersions. "Don't throw off on my new car."

Tight as Dick's hatband: Stingy. It is not known who Dick was or why his hatband was so tight or what any of it has to do with being close with a dollar, but folks down South still say "Him loan you money? He's tight as Dick's hatband."

Til the last pea's out of the dish: To remain at a social gathering for an unconscionably long time. "They'll stay, 'til the last pea's out of the dish."

Tore up: Distraught, very upset. "His wife just left him, and he's all tore up about it."

Toreckly: Later. "You go on ahead. We'll be along toreckly."

Tote: To carry. "Can you tote that big sack of corn meal?"

Tother: One or the other. "You can have this one, or you can take tother one."

Troll: State trooper. "Ah got stopped by the highway troll on I-95."

Twict: One more than once. "Ah've told you once. Ah'm not gonna tell you twict."

U

Ugly: Unpleasant, disagreeable or mean. "Now, Junior, don't you be ugly to your new sister."

Uhmewzin: Funny, comical. "Few things are more uhmewzin than a Yankee tryin' to affect a Suthun accent, since they invariably address one person as 'y'all' when any Suthun six-year-old knows 'y'all' is always plural because it means 'all of you.' "

Uhmurkin: Someone who lives in the United States of Uhmurka. "Thomas Jefferson was a great Uhmurkin."

Unbeknownst: Lacking knowledge of. "Unbeknownst to them, he had marked the cards."

Unnuther: One more. "You want unnuther biscuit?"

Usta: Used to. "Ah usta live in Savannah."

V

Vampar: A fearsome creature that sleeps in a coffin and lives on human blood. "Dracula was a vampar."

Vaymuch: Not a whole lot, when expressed in the negative. "Ah don't like this ham vaymuch."

ViEENer: Small canned sausages. "You want smore viEENers?"

W

Wahn: What Jesus turned the water into, unless you're a Babdist who is persuaded it was only grape juice. "Could Ah have another glass of that wahn?"

Waller: Rolling about, usually done by children and hogs. "Billy, don't you waller all over that bed. Ah jest made it up."

AHH... FRUIT OF THE VINE... WAHN

War: Metal strands attached to fence posts or that carry power over long distances. "Be careful and don't get stuck on that bobwar."

Warsh: To cleanse one's body or dishes, often with the aid of a warshrag, known to Yankees as a washcloth. "Hang up that warshrag when you're done with it."

Waw: A conflict between military forces. "My greatgrandpaw fought in the Waw for Suthun Independence."

Wawk: A method of non-polluting travel by foot. "Why don't we take an old-fashioned wawk?"

Wawl: A partition used to separate rooms. "The wawls in these new apartment buildings sure are thin. Kind of embarrassin' when the people next door are newlyweds."

Wawst: A stinging insect. "Watch out! That's a wawst, and he's mad as a hornet!"

Wear out: An expression used to describe a highly effective method of behavior modification in children. "When Ah get ahold of that boy, Ah'm gonna wear him out."

Wender: A glass-covered opening in a wall. "Open that wender. It's too hot in here."

Wenderlight: A pane of glass. "That baseball went right through the wenderlight."

What: The absence of color. "Mark Twain liked to wear what suits."

Whirl: Where will. "Whirl you spend eternity?" "With my luck, probably in Newark."

Whirr: Where. "Whirr you goin'?"

Whitleather: A durable hide used for making harnesses and employed in speech for comparative purposes. "This steak's as tough as whitleather."

Whup: To beat up or to strike. "If a man kicks my dawg, he'll have to whup me."

Win: An unseen force that propels sailboats. "We're not gittin' anywhere. The win's died down."

Winsheel: What you see through when you drive a car. "Remember when service station attendants used to clean your winsheel?"

Won't: Was not—an eastern North Carolina expression. "Ah didn't do it. It won't me."

Wooden: Would not. "Ah wooden do that if Ah was you."

Wore out: Exhausted, used up. "No use tryin' to fix that washing machine. It's plum wore out."

Wretched: A man's name. "Wretched Burton was a good actor."

Wuf: A fierce wild animal that is closely related to the dog. When they get together it is called a wufpack, which is also the nickname of North Carolina State's athletic teams. "Ah never will forget the time the Wufpack whupped the tar out of UCLA and won the national basketball championship."

Wuk: Something most of us have to do to earn money. "Does he still wuk in Etlanna?"

YANKEE
DIME

Y

Y'all: A useful Southern word that is consistently misused by Northerners when they try to mimic a Southern accent, which they do with appalling regularity. Y'all is always plural because it means you all, or all of you. It is never—repeat, never—used in reference to only one person. At least not by Southerners. "Where y'all goin'?"

Yale: What Confederate soldiers did when they charged. "You wanna hear a Rebel yale?"

Yankee: Anyone who is not from Kentucky, Virginia, Tennessee, North Carolina, South Carolina, Georgia, Florida, Alabama, Mississippi, Louisiana, Arkansas, Texas and possibly Oklahoma and West-by-God-Virginia. A Yankee may become an honorary

Southerner, but a Southerner cannot become a Yankee, assuming any Southerner wanted to. "Momma, can a Yankee go to heaven?" "Don't ask foolish questions, son. Of course not."

Yankee dime: A kiss. "How 'bout a Yankee dime, sugar?"

Yankee shot: A Southern child's navel. "Momma, what's this on my belly?" "That's where the Yankee shot you. That's yo Yankee shot."

Yarbs: Herbs. "Grandmaw's fixin' to make a spring tonic out of roots and yarbs."

Yat: A common greeting in the Irish Channel section of New Orleans. Instead of saying "hey" in lieu of "hello" the way most Southerners do, they say, "Where yat?"

Yeller: One of the primary colors. "A labor union would call this a yeller dawg contrack."

Yesterdee: The day before today. "Where were you yesterdee?"

Yew: Not a tree, but a personal pronoun. "Yew wanna shoot some pool?"

Y'heah?: A redundant expression tacked onto the end of sentences by Southerners. "Y'all come back soon, y'heah?"

Yo: The possessive of you. "What's yo name?"

Yonduh: In a particular direction. "That's a pretty house over yonduh on that hill."

Yontny: Do you want any. "Yontny more corn bread?"

Yore: Another personal pronoun, this one denoting ownership. "Where's yore wife tonight?"

Yungins: Also spelled younguns, meaning young ones. "Ah want all you yungins in bed in five minutes."

Z

Zackly: Precisely. "Ah don't zackly know where he is."

Zat: Is that. "Zat yo dawg?"

Zit: Is it. "Zit already midnight, sugar? Tahm sure flies when you're havin' fun."

Steve Mitchell (1935–1982) was born and raised in North Carolina. He was an editorial writer and humor columnist for the *Palm Beach Post* for ten years. He is survived by his loving daughter, Maria, who still clings to the hope that all Yankees will learn how to talk right.

SCRAWLS aka **Sam C. Rawls** is a Florida cracker and the editorial cartoonist for *The Citizen* newspapers in Georgia. He is a past president of the Association of American Editorial Cartoonists.